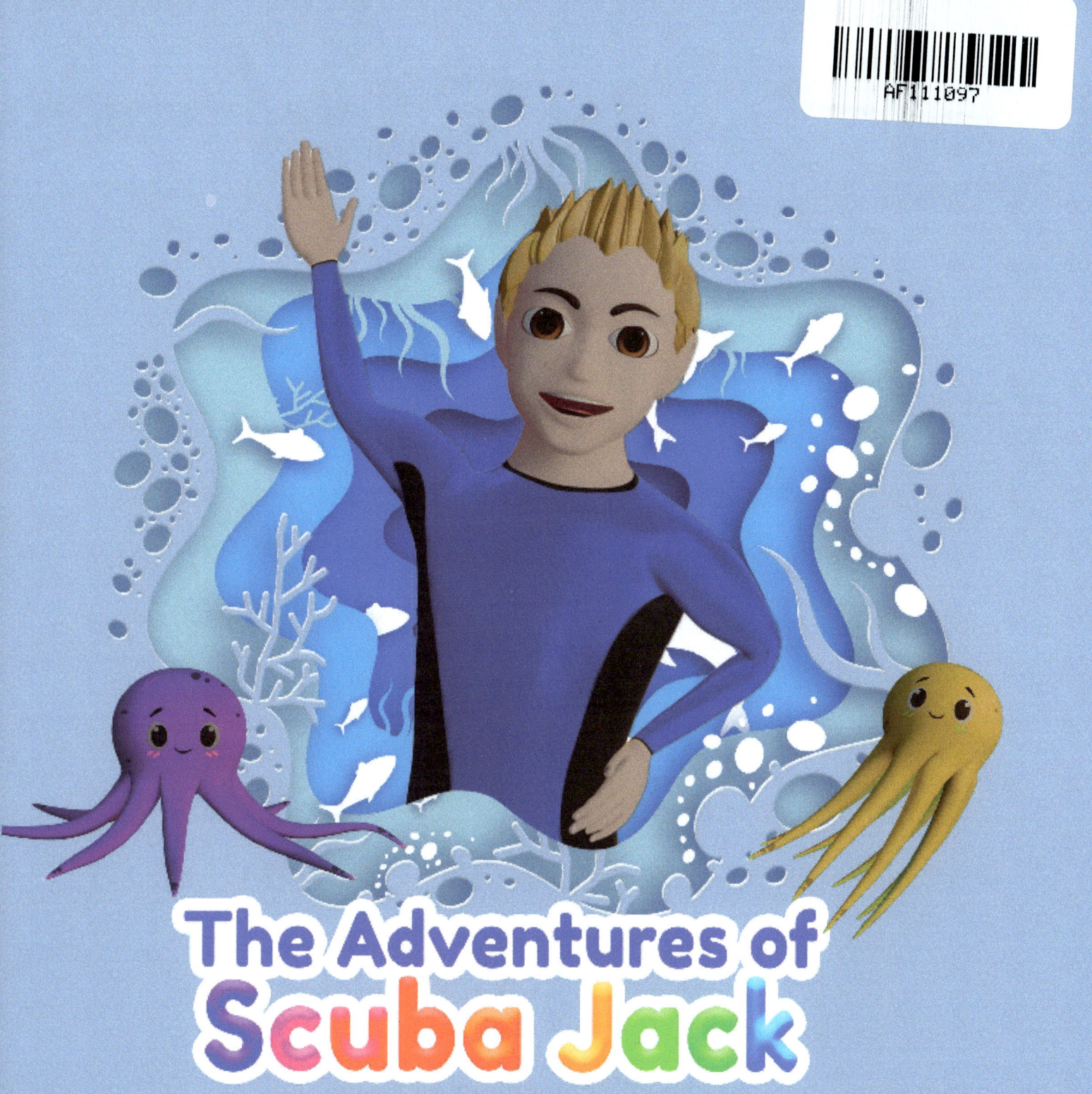

Visit us at
www.adventuresofscubajack.com
for more FUN Learning!

Welcome to the amazing world of sharks! Did you know there are over 500 different species of sharks around the world? These incredible creatures come in all shapes and sizes, from tiny deep-sea dwellers to massive ocean predators. Scientists are still discovering new species, so the exact number continues to grow!

Great White Sharks

The great white shark is one of the biggest and strongest fish in the ocean! It has a big, pointy nose, sharp teeth, and a strong tail that helps it swim super-fast. Great white sharks love to explore the deep blue sea and can jump high out of the water! Even though they look scary, they don't want to bother people; they just like to hunt for fish and sea animals. These amazing sharks have been around for a very long time and are some of the best swimmers in the ocean!

FUN FACT

Great white sharks migrate thousands of miles! Some swim from California to Hawaii or from South Africa to Australia—a journey of over 12,000 miles!

Key Locations Where Great White Sharks Are Found:

Atlantic Ocean:
U.S. East Coast (Massachusetts, Florida, South Carolina), Gulf of Mexico (less common), Canada (Nova Scotia), Europe (Spain, Portugal, and Mediterranean Sea), South Africa (False Bay, Gansbaai – famous for shark cage diving!)

Indian Ocean:
South Africa & Mozambique, Western Australia

Pacific Ocean:
California (Monterey Bay, Farallon Islands, Guadalupe Island, Baja California), Hawaii (occasionally seen), Japan & Taiwan, New Zealand

Hammerhead Sharks

The hammerhead shark is one of the coolest sharks in the ocean! It has a wide, flat head that looks like a hammer, which helps it see all around as it swims. Hammerhead sharks love warm waters and spend their time looking for fish, squid, and little sea creatures to eat. Even though they look different from other sharks, they are great swimmers and very good at finding food. These amazing sharks are fun to watch as they glide through the ocean with their big, wiggly bodies!

FUN FACT

Some hammerhead sharks migrate long distances in groups, especially during the summer. Large schools of hundreds of scalloped hammerheads can be seen near places like the Galápagos Islands and Costa Rica's Cocos Island!

Key Locations Where Hammerhead Sharks Are Found:

Atlantic Ocean:
U.S. East Coast (North Carolina to Florida), Gulf of Mexico & The Caribbean, Brazil & West Africa.

Indian Ocean:
East Africa (Mozambique, Kenya, South Africa), India & Maldives, Australia & Seychelles.

Pacific Ocean:
California & Baja California, Mexico, Galápagos Islands & Ecuador, Indonesia & Philippines, Hawaiian Islands

Tiger Sharks

The tiger shark is a big, strong fish that swims in the ocean! It has stripes on its body, just like a tiger, which is how it got its name. Tiger sharks are very curious and like to explore, using their sharp teeth to eat many kinds of food, like fish, crabs, and even sea turtles! They are great swimmers and can glide through the water with their powerful tails. Even though they might look a little scary, they are just a special part of the big blue ocean!

FUN FACT

Tiger sharks are called the "garbage cans of the sea" because they eat almost anything! Scientists have found unusual objects inside tiger sharks, like license plates, tires, and even a suit of armor!

Key Locations Where Tiger Sharks Are Found:

Atlantic Ocean:
U.S. East Coast (Florida, South Carolina, Gulf of Mexico), Caribbean Sea & The Bahamas (Tiger Beach is famous for tiger sharks!), Brazil & West Africa

Indian Ocean:
South Africa & Madagascar, India & Sri Lanka, Seychelles & Maldives.

Pacific Ocean:
Hawaiian Islands (Commonly seen in Oahu & Maui), Australia (Great Barrier Reef, Western Australia), Indonesia & Philippines, Fiji & Tahiti

Whale Sharks

The whale shark is the biggest fish in the ocean, but don't worry, it's super gentle! Even though it looks huge, it doesn't have sharp teeth like other sharks. Instead, it swims with its big mouth open to scoop up tiny food like plankton and small fish. Whale sharks have beautiful spots all over their bodies, just like a starry night sky. They love swimming in warm waters and are friendly giants of the sea!

FUN FACT

Whale sharks are known to migrate thousands of miles each year to follow plankton blooms, their favorite food! Some travel from Australia to Indonesia or from Mexico to the Philippines.

Key Locations Where Whale Sharks Are Found:

Atlantic Ocean:
U.S. (Gulf of Mexico & Florida), Caribbean Sea (Belize, Honduras, Mexico's Yucatán Peninsula), Brazil & West Africa.

Indian Ocean:
Maldives & Seychelles, India & Sri Lanka, Coast of East Africa (Mozambique, Tanzania, Kenya).

Pacific Ocean:
Australia (Ningaloo Reef, Western Australia), Indonesia & Philippines. Thailand & Vietnam, Galápagos Islands & Mexico's Baja Peninsula

The Greenland Sharks

The Greenland shark is a slow-moving giant that lives in the deep, cold ocean! It swims very slowly and can live for hundreds of years—longer than any other shark! This special shark likes to explore the dark waters near the icy Arctic, where it finds fish and other sea creatures to eat. Even though it moves slowly, it is a great hunter and can sneak up on its food. The Greenland shark is a deep-sea mystery, living a long and quiet life in the cold ocean!

FUN FACT

The Greenland shark is the longest-living vertebrate on Earth, with some individuals estimated to be over 400 years old! Scientists believe some were alive before the Pilgrims landed in America!

Arctic & North Atlantic Oceans:
- Greenland & Iceland (where they get their name)
- Canada (Baffin Bay, Hudson Bay, Gulf of St. Lawrence)
- Norway & Northern Europe
- Alaska & Arctic Russia

The Goblin Sharks

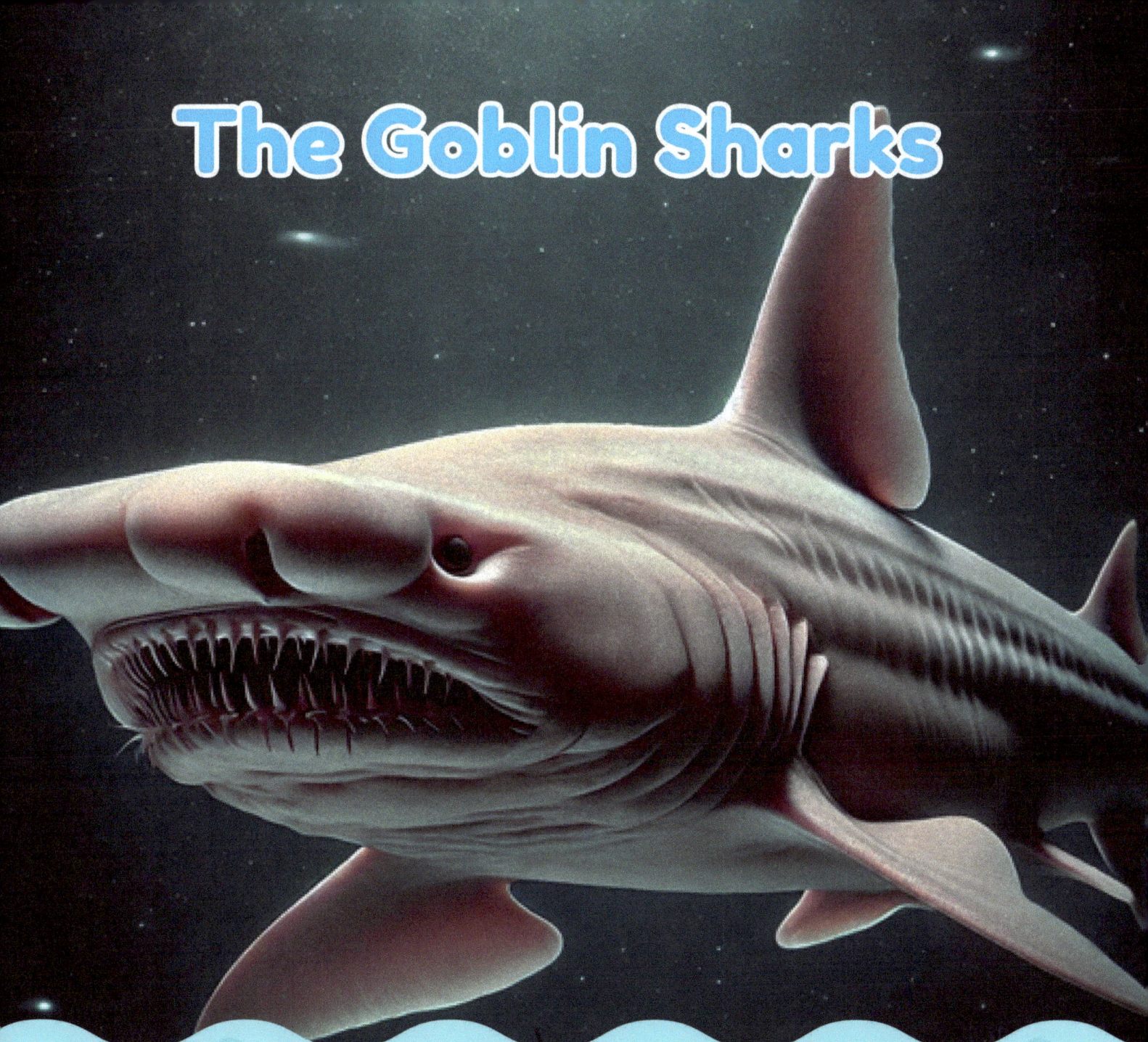

The goblin shark is one of the strangest-looking sharks in the ocean! It has a long, pointy nose and a big mouth that can stretch out to catch fish. This special shark lives deep, deep in the ocean where it is dark and quiet. It has pinkish skin because its body is a little see-through! Even though it looks a little spooky, the goblin shark is a slow swimmer that likes to explore the deep sea, searching for food in the dark waters.

FUN FACT

The goblin shark is sometimes called a "living fossil" because it has barely changed in 125 million years!

Worldwide Deep Oceans

Atlantic Ocean:
Off the coasts of France, Portugal, the U.S. (Gulf of Mexico), and Brazil.

Pacific Ocean:
Japan (where they are most commonly found!), Australia, New Zealand, and California.

Indian Ocean:
South Africa and Mozambique

Black Tip Sharks

The blacktip shark is a fast and playful swimmer that loves warm ocean waters! It gets its name from the black tips on its fins, which make it easy to recognize. Blacktip sharks like to jump out of the water and splash back down, just like a big fishy acrobat! They swim in groups and love to chase little fish for food. Even though they look tough, they are usually shy and like to stay away from people while they explore the ocean!

FUN FACT

Blacktip sharks are known for their spectacular jumps out of the water, often spinning in the air while hunting fish!

Key Locations Where Blacktip Sharks Are Found:

Western Atlantic Ocean:
U.S. East Coast (North Carolina to Florida) Gulf of Mexico, The Bahamas & Caribbean, Brazil & Argentina.

Indian & Pacific Oceans:
South Africa & Madagascar, India & Southeast Asia, Australia (Great Barrier Reef), Indonesia & Papua New Guinea.

Eastern Pacific Ocean:
California & Mexico, Costa Rica & Ecuador.

Basking Sharks

The basking shark is one of the biggest sharks in the ocean, but don't worry—it's super gentle! This giant shark swims with its huge mouth wide open to catch tiny food called plankton. Even though it looks big and scary, it doesn't have sharp teeth and never tries to bite. Basking sharks move slowly through the water, enjoying the sunshine near the surface. They are peaceful giants of the sea, gliding gracefully with their big fins and long bodies!

FUN FACT

Basking sharks migrate long distances! Some travel from Ireland to Africa in winter, looking for better feeding spots.

Some Key Locations Where Basking Sharks Are Found:

North Atlantic Ocean:
Along the coasts of the United States, Canada, Ireland, the UK, and Norway.

Mediterranean Sea:
Occasionally seen in warmer waters.

North Pacific Ocean:
Off the coasts of California, Japan, and British Columbia.

Southern Hemisphere:
Near Argentina, South Africa, and New Zealand.

Leopard Sharks

The leopard shark is a beautiful shark with dark spots all over its body, just like a leopard! It has a long, slender body and loves to swim in shallow, warm waters near sandy beaches and rocky reefs. Leopard sharks are gentle and mostly eat small fish, crabs, and shrimp. They like to swim in groups and are not scary at all! With their pretty patterns and peaceful nature, leopard sharks are one of the friendliest sharks in the ocean!

FUN FACT

Leopard sharks often stay in the same area for years instead of migrating long distances like other sharks!

Key Locations Where Leopard Sharks Are Found:

Eastern Pacific Ocean:
California, USA (especially in San Francisco Bay, Monterey Bay, and Southern California)
- Oregon, USA (though less common)
- Baja California, Mexico

Thresher Sharks

The thresher shark is a fast and powerful swimmer with a very special tail—it's almost as long as its whole body! This shark uses its long, whip-like tail to swat at fish and catch its food. Thresher sharks have big eyes to help them see in deep, dark waters where they love to swim. They are shy and like to stay away from people, gliding gracefully through the ocean. With their sleek bodies and unique tails, thresher sharks are some of the most amazing hunters in the sea!

FUN FACT

Thresher sharks have an incredibly long tail—sometimes as long as their entire body! They use this whip-like tail to stun schools of fish before gobbling them up.

Thresher sharks are found all over the world in both tropical and temperate oceans!

They prefer open waters, usually far from the coast, but sometimes they come closer to shore, especially near continental shelves. You can spot them in places like:

- The Atlantic Ocean
- The Pacific Ocean
- The Indian Ocean

Bull Sharks

The bull shark is a strong and powerful shark that can swim in both salty ocean water and fresh rivers! It has a big, thick body, a short, round nose, and sharp teeth to help it catch fish and other sea creatures. Bull sharks are very good swimmers and can live in places where most sharks cannot, like lakes and rivers. They are curious and like to explore their surroundings, making them one of the most adventurous sharks in the ocean!

FUN FACT

Bull sharks have special kidneys that help them adjust to different types of water, allowing them to swim up rivers and even live in lakes.

The major oceans where bull sharks are found include:
- Atlantic Ocean
- Pacific Ocean
- Indian Ocean

Bull sharks are also unique because they can swim in freshwater, so they are found in rivers and lakes like:
- Amazon River
- Mississippi River
- Lake Nicaragua

Sand Devil Sharks

The sand devil shark is a special kind of shark that likes to rest on the sandy ocean floor. It has a flat body and wide fins that help it hide in the sand, just like a secret underwater ninja! This shark is very good at staying still and waiting for small fish to swim by so it can catch them for dinner. Even though it looks a little different from other sharks, the sand devil is a quiet and clever hunter that loves the deep, peaceful ocean.

FUN FACT

One unusual fact about the sand devil shark is that it looks more like a stingray than a typical shark!

Sand devil sharks, which belong to the angel shark family, are found in the western Atlantic Ocean, primarily along the coast of the United States, from North Carolina to the Gulf of Mexico, and even as far south as Argentina. They prefer sandy or muddy ocean floors in shallow coastal waters and can often be found lying still, camouflaged in the sand, waiting to ambush prey.

Lemon Sharks

Here is a world map highlighting the regions where the lemon shark is commonly found, including the coastal waters of the Atlantic Ocean, the Gulf of Mexico, and the eastern Pacific Ocean.

The lemon shark is a friendly-looking shark with a yellowish-brown body that helps it blend in with the sandy ocean floor. It lives in warm, shallow waters near coral reefs and mangroves, where it hunts for fish, crabs, and small sea creatures. Lemon sharks are social and often swim together in groups. They have a strong sense of smell and excellent eyesight, which help them find food. Even though they can grow quite big, they are not aggressive and prefer to glide peacefully through the ocean!

FUN FACT

Lemon sharks don't swim far from shore, so they are one of the easiest sharks to study in the wild!

Lemon sharks have a special ability—they can "walk" on the ocean floor using their fins!

Mako Sharks

The mako shark is one of the fastest sharks in the ocean! With its sleek, torpedo-shaped body and powerful tail, it can swim at incredible speeds, reaching up to 45 miles per hour. This speedy predator has a sharp, pointed snout and big, sharp teeth that help it catch fish like tuna and swordfish. Its metallic blue top and white belly help it blend into the water as it hunts. Mako sharks are strong and smart swimmers, making them some of the most exciting sharks to see in the wild!

FUN FACT

Super Sharp Teeth – Their teeth are so sharp and pointy that they sometimes poke out of their mouths, making them look extra fierce!

Sharks are a group of fish that have skeletons made of cartilage, five to seven gills, and pectoral fins what are not fused to the head.
- There are 500 species of sharks.
- There is evidence that early sharks may date back to more than 420 million years ago.

Some sharks give live birth and some lay eggs. Shark babies are called pups.

Remoras and pilot fish are fish that attach themselves to sharks and feed on bits of prey as the shark feeds.

Sharks have extremely keen senses that help them find prey.

Sharks have several rows of teeth. When a shark loses a tooth, it will be replaced by a new one. Some sharks lose 10,000 or more teeth in their life.

FUN FACT

Great white sharks migrate thousands of miles! Some swim from California to Hawaii or from South Africa to Australia—a journey of over 12,000 miles!

Great White Sharks are the largest predatory fish on the planet. They can detect a drop of blood in water up to 3 miles away and can jump up to 10 feet out of the water.

Some early sharks were enormous. One of them was the Megalodon.

Shark eggs are covered by a tough, leathery membrane sometimes called a mermaid's purse.
Here is an illustration of a shark egg (mermaid's purse) with the correct dark brown to black coloration and leathery texture.

Sharks have several rows of teeth when a tooth breaks or gets dull, another tooth moves up to replace it.

Ss

Ss is for Shark

shark

S S S S S

s s s s s

Ss Ss Ss Ss

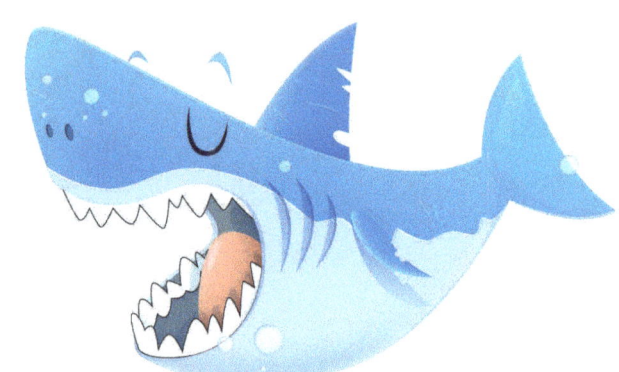

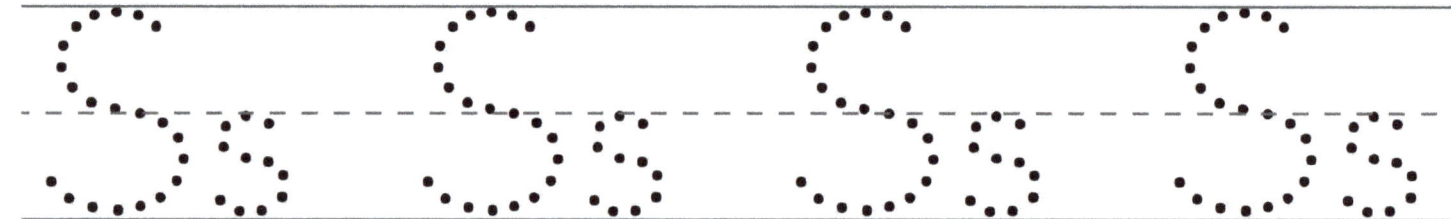

Color it!

Shark Puzzle

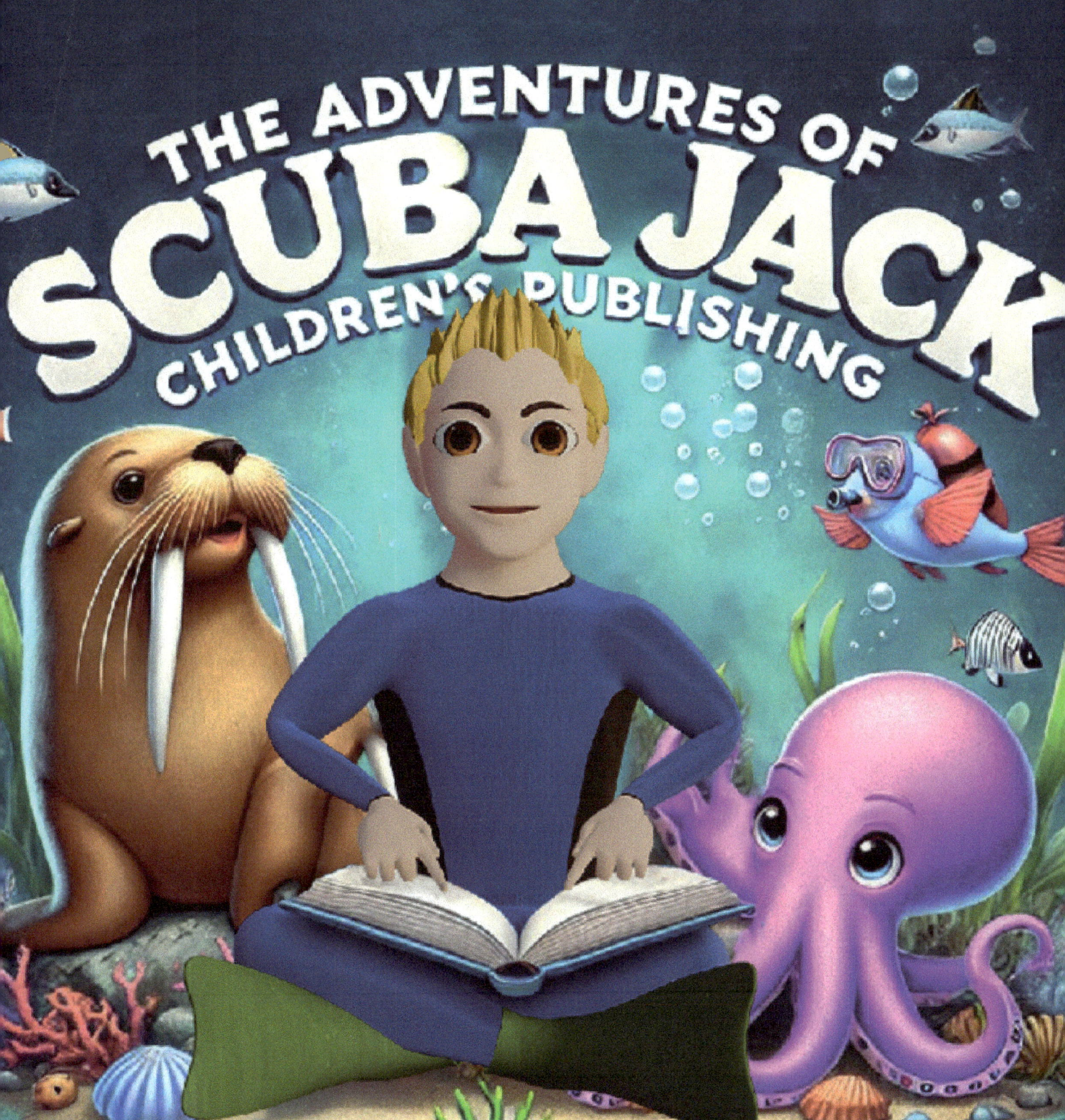

www.ingramcontent.com/pod-product-compliance
Lightning Source LLC
LaVergne TN
LVHW072130060526
838201LV00071B/5004